MATHEW BRADY
Photographing the Civil War

BY STEVEN OTFINOSKI

Celebration Press
Pearson Learning Group

Contents

Introduction

Famed photographer Mathew Brady

Mathew Brady may be the best-known photographer in United States history. He was one of the first photographers to record history as it was being made.

Yet surprisingly little is known about the life of this important man. We are not even sure of the year of his birth. Born in 1823 or 1824 in Warren County, New York, Brady was a quiet man who kept neither a journal nor a diary. Only his remarkable photographs remain to speak for him today.

A NEW INVENTION

In 1826, when Mathew Brady was three or four years old, the world's first known photograph was taken. The person who took it was a French inventor named Joseph Niépce (pronounced nyeps). However, photography did not begin with Niépce. It resulted from discoveries over hundreds of years.

By the early 1800s there was a great demand for pictures, especially portraits. But most people could not afford to have portraits painted by artists. Some scientists hoped to find an inexpensive way to provide the much-wanted pictures. They began experimenting with such materials as paper and metals, which they coated with different kinds of light-sensitive chemicals.

In 1816, Niépce constructed a type of camera from a jewel box and a microscope lens. He experimented for about ten years before discovering how to produce a permanent image with it.

At last he tried putting a **pewter** plate coated with a type of **asphalt** into the camera and exposing the plate, or subjecting it to light, for about eight hours. Then Niépce's picture began to appear. It was a view of a courtyard as seen from his window.

Louis Daguerre

In the 1830s a French artist, Louis Daguerre (dah GAIR), improved Niépce's invention. The two had worked together briefly before Niépce died in 1833.

Daguerre treated sheets of silver-coated copper with **iodine** to make them sensitive to light. He next exposed them in a camera. Then he developed the sheets with **vapors** that rose from heating mercury. Finally Daguerre made his picture permanent with a solution of common salt.

This process required only about 20 to 30 minutes of light exposure and created clearer, sharper pictures. These early photographs, called "**daguerreotypes**," soon became very popular in Europe.

An early daguerreotype. People had to stay perfectly still to get a clear picture.

People in the United States also became interested in Daguerre's invention. One of the first Americans to learn how to make daguerreotypes was Samuel F.B. Morse.

Morse was an artist and the inventor of the telegraph and Morse code, used to send messages by telegraph. On a trip to France in 1839, Morse heard about Daguerre's work and then met with him. Daguerre showed Morse his copper-plate pictures, which greatly interested Morse.

On his return to the United States that same year, Morse set up a studio in New York City for making daguerreotypes. About 1840 he began to teach Daguerre's method of photography. One of his eager students was Mathew Brady.

At about 16, Brady had left home to look for work in Saratoga, New York. There he met William Page, a portrait artist, who became his teacher and friend. Soon both Page and Brady moved to New York City, where Page opened a studio and Brady worked in a store and studied art.

One day Page visited his friend Morse and introduced Brady to him. Morse showed them the daguerreotypes. Brady, in particular, was fascinated. He began to study with Morse and learned how to make daguerreotypes. Photography soon became Brady's passion.

In 1844 he opened his first photography studio in New York City. He worked day and night taking portraits of people. Brady was soon one of the country's most successful photographers.

However, Brady wasn't satisfied with taking pictures of ordinary people. He wanted to record for history the great people of his time.

"From the first," he said, "I regarded myself as under obligation to my country to preserve the faces of its historic men and mothers."

PHOTOGRAPHER OF PRESIDENTS

In February 1849, Brady became the first photographer to be welcomed to the White House. He photographed President James Polk there on Valentine's Day. The President wrote in his diary that day: "I yielded to the request of an artist named Brady, of New York, by sitting for my daguerreotype likeness today."

If Polk looks stiff in his portrait, there is a good reason. People sitting for photographs at that time had to stay perfectly still for up to 40 seconds. If they moved, the picture would be ruined.

Later that year Brady photographed the new President, Zachary Taylor, and his cabinet. By then Brady had opened a studio in the capital.

Brady's 1849 portrait of President James Polk

A daguerreotype photograph was just one copper plate. But Brady soon learned about new ways to make copies of his pictures. In 1850 he worked with writer Charles E. Lester and artist Francis D'Avignon (da veen YOHN). D'Avignon made **lithographs** from Brady's daguerreotpyes of famous Americans. Lithographs are prints made from flat stones or metal plates onto which pictures have been copied. Lester wrote a short biography to go with each lithograph. The first series of 12 portraits was called the Gallery of Illustrious Americans. Among the people pictured were President Zachary Taylor, explorer John Charles Fremont, and wildlife artist John J. Audubon.

In 1856, Scottish photographer Alexander Gardner went to work for Brady. Gardner knew a photographic process called "the wet plate process." It was a great improvement over the daguerreotype. A glass plate was coated with a sticky liquid called **collodion**. The plate was exposed in a camera and then developed, making a **negative**. From this negative any number of photographs could be made on paper.

Soon Brady's wet plate photographs were appearing in such national magazines as *Harper's Weekly*. In 1858 he opened his National Photographic Art Gallery in Washington, D.C., on Pennsylvania Avenue.

Abraham Lincoln, photographed by Mathew Brady in 1860 when Lincoln was running for president

On February 27, 1860, Brady photographed a politician from Illinois who was running for president. His name was Abraham Lincoln. Brady took the picture the day that Lincoln spoke to an audience at the Cooper Union, a school in New York City.

Brady's portrait of Lincoln appeared in *Harper's Weekly* and other magazines. It was the first look at Lincoln that many Americans had. How candidates looked was important even then, and Brady had tried to make Lincoln's appearance as appealing as possible in the photo, smoothing his wrinkled suit and arranging his loose collar to conceal his long neck. When Lincoln was elected president, he gave full credit to the photographer. "Brady and the Cooper Institute made me president," he said.

THE HORRORS OF WAR

In April 1861 the Civil War broke out between the North and the South. The Southern states had seceded, or broken away, from the United States over the issue of slavery.

Mathew Brady wanted to organize a group of photographers to make a photographic record of the war. Friends warned him of the dangers, but Brady felt that it was his mission. He said later, "A spirit in my feet said, 'Go,' and I went."

First he went to President Lincoln to get approval. He also asked Lincoln for special passes for his photographers to visit the battle lines.

Lincoln gave Brady permission to follow the war, but no funding. Brady would have to pay for this huge project out of his own pocket. Although he realized it would be both expensive and dangerous, he hired dozens of photographers to take pictures at different outposts along the battlefront.

He bought old delivery trucks to carry the photographers and their heavy chemicals and camera equipment. The wagons were closed off to light to serve as darkrooms for developing the wet plate photographs. Soldiers were puzzled by these strange wagons. They called them "What-is-it?" wagons.

In July 1861, Brady personally went to photograph the first Battle of Bull Run in Virginia, about 30 miles southwest of Washington, D.C. This was the first major battle of the Civil War. Brady's wagon was overturned in the hurried retreat of the Union army, and most of the photographic equipment was ruined. But a few photos survived the disaster, and they were published in newspapers. One newspaper writer said of them, "There is nothing to compare with them in their powerful contrast of light and shade."

This Mathew Brady photograph of dead soldiers after the Battle of Antietam shocked the public.

At that time taking pictures of the actual fighting between armies during a war presented a major problem for photographers. Exposure of the glass plates still took several seconds inside the camera. To get a clear picture, the people, horses, and equipment being photographed could not move during that time. Therefore, photographs of battle scenes blurred and did not come out well.

In an effort to avoid this problem, Brady and his photographers usually took two major kinds of photographs during the Civil War. One kind was of the battlefield after the battle ended, showing the dead and wounded soldiers.

In September 1862, Alexander Gardner, Brady, and other assistants photographed dead soldiers after the Battle of Antietam. It was one of the bloodiest battles of the war. When the pictures appeared in *Harper's Weekly*, the public was shocked to see the hundreds of dead bodies lying on the battlefield. Never before had a photograph shown the terrible violence of war.

Brady's stark photographs brought the war's horrors home to the American people. He displayed the photographs in his New York gallery and called the exhibit "The Dead of Antietam."

This Brady photograph shows Civil War soldiers at camp in Michigan.

The other kind of photograph Brady and his assistants liked to take was of soldiers at camp. Sometimes they photographed entire regiments of soldiers standing at attention. Other pictures showed what camp life was like for the ordinary soldier. Small groups of men posed and were photographed cooking food, doing other chores, or simply relaxing.

For the first time, people saw war as it really was. The results of the fighting were bloody and grim. Yet between battles, life could be somewhat ordinary, even boring.

Though his eyesight was growing weaker, Brady went to several of the bloodiest battles and took many pictures himself. But it was not possible for him to take all the photos in his huge collection personally. Many were taken by Alexander Gardner and the other photographers Brady had hired. Brady organized the work and supervised his assistants both at the studio and on the battlefields.

Sometimes he needed photographs of events his group was unable to cover. Then Brady bought them from other photographers. These photographs also became part of Brady's collection. As was common at that time, all the war photos in his collection were credited "Photograph by Brady," even though they were the work of many people.

According to some historians, Gardner was unhappy with not getting credit for his work and left Brady in 1863. Others say that the break resulted from a disagreement over Gardner's wages. For whatever reason, Gardner opened his own studio and continued to photograph war scenes. Later he published a collection of his photographs of the war.

By now still other photographers were competing with Brady in photographing the war. However, the sharp, clear pictures taken by Brady and his first group continue to be the most famous.

PHOTOGRAPHING THE WAR'S HEROES

Brady's 1864 portrait of Union General Ulysses S. Grant at camp in Cold Harbor, Virginia

During the war, Brady was still interested in photographing famous people. He took pictures of many Union generals and officers. For example, in 1864 he photographed General Ulysses S. Grant, Commander in Chief of the Union armies. Brady photographed Grant first in the studio and later where his army was camped.

Brady had received Grant's permission to travel behind the battle lines earlier that year. Some say Brady's wife had spoken to Mrs. Grant, who helped persuade her husband to let Brady go wherever he wanted to.

In early 1865, in a series of Union victories, Grant's soldiers forced the Confederate troops to retreat farther and farther south. General Robert E. Lee became commander in chief of all Confederate armies in February 1865. By that time the Confederacy, short of soldiers and supplies, was nearing defeat.

On April 9, 1865, General Lee surrendered to General Grant at Appomattox Courthouse, in south central Virginia. The two generals met in a private house to discuss terms for the surrender. The long, hard conflict was finally at an end.

No photograph was taken of the actual surrender. Brady was taking photographs in the area and came at once when he heard the news. He was able to photograph only the private house, now empty!

A few days later Brady went to Lee's home in Richmond, Virginia, and asked Lee to sit for his photograph. Lee had known Brady for many years. At first Lee said no, but coaxed by his wife and friends, he finally agreed.

"It was supposed that after his defeat it would be preposterous to ask him to sit," said Brady years later, "but I thought that to be the time for the historical picture."

President Abraham Lincoln's funeral procession down Pennsylvania Avenue

The joy of the Union victory soon turned to great sorrow. On April 14, 1865, actor John Wilkes Booth shot President Lincoln at Ford's Theater in Washington, D.C. Unconscious, Lincoln was taken to a boarding house across the street. Through the night, doctors tried to save his life, but Lincoln died at 7:22 the next morning.

Later Brady worked with artist Alonzo Chappel to create a memorial painting. Each person present the night Lincoln died went later to Brady's studio and was photographed. Chappel then drew the people from the photos. From the drawings, he created the well-known painting *The Last Hours of Lincoln*.

A Gamble Lost

Mathew Brady believed he was meant to make a photographic history of the Civil War. In order to do so, he spent $100,000 of his own money, a fortune at that time.

After the war Brady had a huge number of photographs and negatives. There were so many that they were stored in warehouses, which was also expensive. Brady expected that the government, museums, and private citizens would want to buy his pictures.

But Americans were tired of war and cruelty and death. They saw Brady's war photographs as reminders of events they would rather forget. Although many legislators believed that the photographs were of such historic importance that they should belong to the government, Congress was not willing to buy the photographs at that time. Most of the collection remained unsold.

Brady was broke and in debt. He dismissed his teams of photographers and sold some property in New York City. In 1868 he was forced to sell his gallery in Washington to pay debts. However, he continued to work in a smaller studio, photographing important events and people around him.

Portrait of poet Walt Whitman

One of those people was the poet Walt Whitman. The two men had a lot in common. Both were born and raised in New York. Both moved to Washington and lived there during the Civil War. While Brady photographed scenes of the war, Whitman worked as a nurse, caring for the wounded, and wrote a volume of Civil War poems.

Whitman and Brady were friends, and Brady photographed Whitman on several occasions. "We had many a talk together," Whitman recalled years later. He went on to praise Brady's idea of making a photographic history. Whitman felt that photographs show a more accurate history than books by historians who disagree with one another.

Also in 1868, Brady photographed some members of Congress who were making history. In an ongoing conflict with Congress, the new President, Andrew Johnson, had dismissed a Cabinet member without notifying the Senate. In an effort to remove Johnson from office, the House of Representatives **impeached** him. That is, they brought charges of wrongdoing against him, and his impeachment trial was held in the Senate. Johnson was the first president in U.S. history to be impeached.

During the impeachment proceedings, Brady photographed the impeachment committee in his Washington studio. Before one of their meetings, they posed for a group photograph, which was then printed in several newspapers. The photo gave the American people a chance to look at the men who were involved in this historic event.

The impeachment trial lasted about two months. In the end the Senate failed to convict Johnson by just one vote.

During earlier and happier times, Brady had also photographed Andrew Johnson. Other subjects for Brady's camera were Native American Chief Red Cloud and his men, following their visit to the White House, and Clara Barton, founder of the American Red Cross.

In 1873 the country was in financial crisis. Mathew Brady filed for bankruptcy. Anthony and Company, Brady's supplier during the war, now pressed him for payment, so he gave the company some of his valuable photographic plates to pay part of the debt.

Congress still showed no interest in buying his Civil War collection. But in 1874 the owners of the warehouse where a large number of his Civil War plates were stored put them up for auction. Brady couldn't pay the $2,840 he owed in storage fees. The buyer, who paid just the storage fees, was the U.S. government! It now had possession of those plates but not the title, or legal rights, to them.

Brady's friends in Congress felt the government had taken advantage of him. Representative James A. Garfield, future president of the United States, helped get Congress to pay Brady $25,000 for full title to those plates that were already in a government warehouse. Brady received the money in 1875, most of which went to pay debts.

To make matters worse, his wife became seriously ill. When she died in 1887, it was a terrible blow. The course of his life continued downhill. In Washington in 1895, a streetcar pulled by horses struck Brady, breaking his leg. After he recovered, he moved to New York City and started work on a lecture series. But Brady became ill and died there in 1896, alone and almost forgotten.

About 1900, Anthony and Company sold the Brady negatives it owned to Frederick Hill Meserve, an amateur historian. In 1981 the Meserve family sold the collection. The National Portrait Gallery bought about 5,000 of Brady's negatives.

Today these photographs have been reprinted in books and magazines and shown in galleries. Many of Brady's portraits can still be seen in the National Portrait Gallery. His photographs of the Civil War and of famous Americans provide a pictorial record of an important part of our country's history.

If you visit the National Portrait Gallery in Washington, D.C., you can see many of Brady's photographs.

Mathew Brady's Civil War photographs were a turning point in the art of photography. Before that time, photography was seen mostly as a business. Afterward, because of Brady's great skill with the camera, it was seen as a form of art.

The way he posed his subjects and the way he used lighting and background produced photographs that reveal the subjects' most important qualities. Brady kept up with the latest developments in photography and used the newest techniques.

Brady's photographs mark the first time anyone had documented a war in pictures. His Civil War photographs are the first images of war shot on American soil. Since that time, **photojournalists** have recorded nearly every major war and news event in the world.

We owe a great debt to Mathew Brady and the brave men who worked with him. Perhaps he himself said it best. "The camera is the eye of history . . . you must never make bad pictures."